The Sailors of the Skies

The Paper Drafts

Onie Maniego

The Sailors of the Skies

Third Edition

ISBN: 9798610623160

The Paper Drafts is a collection of art, poetry, and fiction.

The Sailors of the Skies desires to experience nostalgia and to contemplate the little things in life. Satiate your soul with the fires of summer, delve into the river of time and sail into the depths of the heavens.

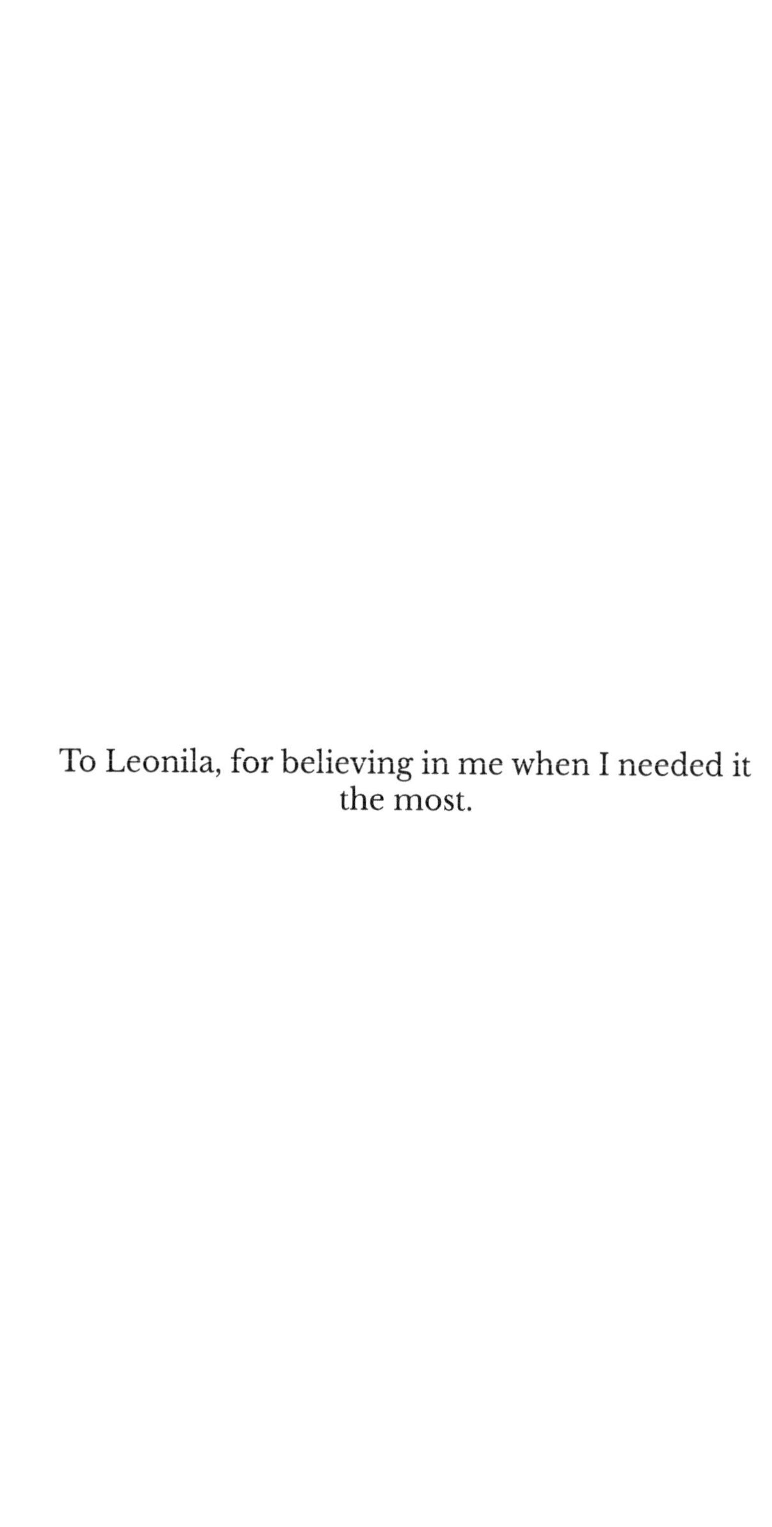

To Leonila, for believing in me when I needed it
the most.

ACKNOWLEDGMENTS

To write a book alone for oneself is possible, but to create a book for others, it was only possible with the help of these people.

I would like to thank Rodney and Marisa, my parents, for trusting me in the decisions I make and for inspiring me to do more in life.

I would also want to give thanks to Rose, Jane, and Dawn, my siblings, for the believing in my goals and for the countless encouragement and support they give to me.

This wouldn't also be possible without ma'am Rhodora Bande, my former teacher. She had greatly influenced me to continue writing and helped me find my niche.

CONTENTS

The Fires of Summer
Part I

Sunshine

I woke up and the sun peeked,
I walked in a late morning stroll,
And when she blinked, I was gone.
I went out again and now she's asleep.

Summery Day

This day was like his childhood days,
The blue skies were peaceful and calm.
The clouds rested on the horizons,
As the sun rays flickered—warm and golden.
The gentle breeze brushed on his skin.
The good old days,
The roads burnt and dusty.
Shadows were crisp on the dry ground.
The Camias tree still stood,
Its leaves chiming by the wind.
The Pineapples basked under the sun,
With all its leaves pointing to the sky.
He goes out to see the summery day.
There was no one outside,
Was the sun still high?

The River that Waters the Fields

Time swings the hammock,
Like the breeze
On a late dry season.
Or it may be El Niño,
Still, the ground is wet,
As the mountains are blessed.
The brook still flows
And the fields are fat.

Misty Trail in Mid-April

Knees lift and feet landed
On wet ground
Covered with foliage
And dewdrops.

Uphill, along the thicket,
Twigs and leaves
Lead to another trail—
danger on one side.

Rocks turned to boulders,
Downhill, the heart is racing
And the stream is gushing,
Chilly tune of the river nymph.

Glug-glug, the water flows
From the underground,
Sweet water cascades
Into the rocky river.

Mist showered,
As light as a feather
And as thin as air
On a sunny noon.

Red flower bathed,
Petals covered in dew
And roots embracing
The mossy rock.

Caballero

(To Rose Maniego)
Summer silently burn in warm fires,
The unheard laughter of early May,
Yearning for the clouds and storms,
For the heavens to touch the earth.

Dry Season on Mid-May

Summer has peaked,
Giving intense heat,
Humid air and warm breeze
Wrapped gently on dry ground.

Stuck on a dusty road,
Along unfamiliar faces
And stolen glances—
Time slacked off.

Sun after one o'clock
Gave weary countenance,
Passengers fan themselves,
Wiping sweat after sweat.

Past along the Caballero trees,
Adorned in fiery blossoms,
Casting crisp shadows—
Dying leaflets rained over.

Summer Fields

Sing with the souls of wildflowers,
Carry them away in the gushing pains
To hear their forsaken murmurs
And to rest in the turbulent fires.

Sweet petals follow my thirst,
Come die in the path I'm taking
To bloom the colors of May
And burn in crimson and gold.

In the deathbed bloom in multitude,
Sip the emptiness inside me
To send notes of the dying flowers
And awaken those who longed for love.

Dance by the light of death,
In forms of blazing wildflowers
To lay awake until my demise
And meet me at the edges of dawn.

When Golds Grew on Trees

Summery scent,
Of damp clay and grasses,
On humid mornings
And hot afternoons.

Plump and green,
Nurtured in rich soil,
Bore from love and labor—
Trees bent down to the ground.

Hand-picked,
Select of seasoned-hands,
Wrapped away from light,
Until yellow as the sun.

Tease me,
By your orange and yellows,
Fed by tart and sweet pulp—
A taste of blessed earth.

Fires of Summer

Like grasses we die in the sun's fires
While waiting for the clouds to rain,
We sang in the scent of dust
To hear the thirst of the fallen.

We fade unto our deathbeds,
Burnt from the memories of the past,
Hear our longing of the storms
And bring its floods into the hearts.

Hopes ablaze in fires of summer,
Fallen in thousand leaves of gold,
Embracing the ground of its pieces,
To sleep until the rivers, flow again.

Let the storms brew from the horizons
And feed the skies in darkness,
So, when the rain water the fields,
We shall awaken and live again.

Golden Rain

Midday sun blossoms in tantalizing hues,
Hear its forsaken voices of age-old tunes;
Heavenly shower cried in golden tears—
A marmalade rain of fallen memories.

Wedelia

(To Dawn Maniego)
Drops of sun bloom in silence,
Awake in the valleys and hills;
Little flowers of yellow and gold,
Sing the songs of the hills.

Summer in October

A lifetime swallowed me whole,
Gulped in warm jades and marigolds;
Quenched by the bubbles of the ripe earth,
Bursting in saccharine tang of October.

Dragonflies

Along with the clouds I see,
Something flying above me.
It has wings but are not butterflies.
It has a tail but are not birds.
On the bright sky,
Sometimes, on the bushes.
Sometimes, above the pineapple garden.
Try to reach it,
So high, but you can't reach the dragonflies.

Sky

If I gaze into the skies,
A lot of things I start to ponder,
But I feel comfort and peace.
I can close my eyes
And breathe
The sweet wind,
And let the cozy breeze
brush onto my skin.

The Sailors of the Skies

Journey of the Clouds
Part II

Lonely Days

I just want to sit on this bench,
While watching the sad skies.
I'll wait for the rain,
And listen to the thunder.

The Journey of the Clouds

I laid on the cold grass,
And I was a giant to an ant.
I gazed into the skies,
And I felt so small.
I raised my hand with might,
Trying to reach the stars.

I dreamt to touch the clouds,
Like the trees had tried in years.
I shivered by the breeze,
When the remnants of the western sea
Missed the mountains.

I followed the swift clouds,
As it flew hastily to the west.
I gazed on the ones
That are like blades or feathers,
As it faded in a moment.
I peeked at the solitary ones,
As it moved at a slowly.

I waited for the others
That looked like
The waves of the sea,
And have journeyed to the north.
I blinked for a second,
While the stars and the moon
Unknowingly sailed to the west.

Thunder

The weather was hot,
Then it was not.
There were stars,
And now there was none.
There are clouds and lightning,
Then thunders rolls.

A Nutty Scent of Dust

All the insects came to rest,
As the clouds drifts to the west.
All the mist showered so fast,
Then, came a nutty scent of dust.

I Was Once a Cloud

I was once a speck at birth
And was invisible like the stars at noon.
I woke up at the zenith of the earth
And was as high as the moon.
I gobbled some moist air
Then made waves across the sky.
I was as huge as a bear
But could only shout a lullaby.
I felt cold, so I curled away
And lazed on an afternoon sun.
I saw the town was gray
But I enjoyed having a tan.
I could already tell
That I was feeling weak.
I wasn't feeling well,
So, I docked on the mountain peak.
I closed my eyes
And laid on the hills and plain.
I, then bade goodbyes,
As I disappeared after the rain.

Sudden Shower on an Early Morning

Rain! Oh, sweet rain!
Down my window pane.
The ground is already wet,
But the ground is dry, I bet.

Rain! Oh, mellow shower!
Rolling upon the morning flowers.
And the sun's warm rays came out,
The birds will be happy, no doubt.

A Cloud's Melancholy

I heard the wind,
It sighed.
Oh! Dear clouds,
Why did you cry?

I saw the trees—
Now asleep.
Oh! Dear clouds,
Why did you weep?

Mist

I walked beneath the flame trees,
While the mist silently started,
As it rained upon the grasses
And showered the pavement.

Battle of the Celestial Archers

Ashen sailcloth in rare linen—
A fleet of thousand warships
Invading through the celestial sea
In its cerulean waters.

Herculean artillery
Awaiting at the tropical coast.
Roar! Deathly streak of hot cannonball
Launched from the heavens.

Thunderous drum-rolls
Echoed along with the marching sounds.
Archers sent a spindrift of arrows,
Drenching the land in rain.

Why I Hated Rainy Days

When the lighting
Sparks from afar,
The thunder whispers
Through the mild rain.

Clouds are heavy,
Leaves are teary,
And the ground
Is flooded.

Twigs afloat
On muddy puddles.
Birds hid in trees and roofs.

Houses fade
Behind the white rain.

I was, too,
Covered under blankets,
Watching the saddened skies.

With the tiny hands,
Held around a bowl
Of hot porridge.

The rain was sweet as sugar,
Bitter as cocoa, and
Mild like cereal.

The Sound of Rain

Remember when you
Could touch the clouds,
When you could tiptoe
In the white rain shower?

You could hear
The sky drizzling
On everyone,
When the greens
Cannot see each other.

See the dancing birds
Behind the mesmerizing streaks
Of the rain,
As the shivering wind
Embraced the buildings.

The lightning flickered
On the dark noon,
While the thunder paraded through
The vague horizon.

Tap. Tap. Tap.
And soon, it knocked
On the crystal-clear wall.

Cold Embrace

Thousand rains shove
Unto every soul,
But I never heard
A whistling howl.
As white
As the heavy clouds,
Tempered winds struck
Unto the western bounds.
Soft hands of
The gentle storm brushed by.
Her bittersweet song,
Serenaded the afternoon sky.

Like an eagle
I sat on the peak,
Holding my weight,
As I clenched on a brick.
My wrinkled hide,
I cannot see—
As vague as the future
To foresee.
I was flying
And steadily rising
From the deep sea,
And unto the surface, at last!

The very last downpour
Leapt to die on earth,
Hitting on leaves in all its worth—
In every tree at the distant hills.
With every bone in chills,
I shook then flew.

Evening Rain

How mesmerizing the evening rain is?
If words can only describe how wonderful it is.
Like how it blurs things at a distance.
Like how it makes dull objects shine.
Like how the cold the wind is.
Like how the thin drops of rain hits the ground.
Like how it waters the thirsty earth.

Midnight Rain

Hey night sky, why so sad?
The streetlights are fuzzy
And the road is flooded.
I walked alone
Under your splashing tears.
I wonder what made you cry.

November Nights

When the rain begins at night,
Pull the clouds on your window pane,
Its strings rolled into your palms,
And the tears kept in sealed jars.

Let the lightning hit your heart,
Burning the memories of warm nights.
Sing the notes of its thunders,
As your thoughts fade with the rain.

When the candle ceases its life,
Find the shadows of the beasts,
The footsteps haunting in your sleep,
And its whispers, cold as the wind.

Let the storm sing its lullabies,
Calming the shouting of your soul.
Rest by the fading sound of rain,
As the moon released into the sky.

A Morning in December

All night it rained.
Saturday morning came,
But alarm goes off.
Still, I dozed off.

The Cursed Storm

Her screeching gale
Sent a heavy rainfall,
Flaunting a robe of darkness
In metallic gray.

Chilly rage
Of a terrible rainstorm;
Her familiar sobbing—
the sound of the centennial typhoon!

Flood rose at her command,
Uprooted trees bowed in fear.
But her voice mysteriously gone,
The, abruptly sent another howling gust.

When she was done,
Left an inaudible encore;
Brought a horde of leafless trees—
And a diminished island!

The Raging Seas
Part III

The Raging Seas

The unknown seas ravaged my voyage,
Sailing through the menacing waves
Where sea ghosts dine in sailor's souls,
Blinding me by its complete darkness.

The gargantuan waves danced in euphoria,
Summoning a portal of dysphoria
Where wrathful serpents clash in war dance,
Tormenting me in seasickness.

The dark heavens lit in lilac hues,
Tracing zigzag lines toward the waters
Where the mouths of the dragons lay open,
Haunting me its split-second marvel.

The tempestuous storm howled in anger,
Blasting screeching thunder and rain
Where empyrean beasts brawl to death,
Drowning me in lost hope to reach the harbor.

Treasure Island

From afar 'twas like the adventures of a hero,
Beside me are swords of golden lights,
Streaking behind the horizon.
Ahead of me is a vast loot,
Glimmering like gold across the western sky—
Dotted by emeralds, rubies and peridots!

Old Islands

Pearls afloat on the seas
On the distant waves of the past.
Fishes escape in midair flight,
Far into the edges of life.

Waves of time tugged the souls
Where the heavens await them,
As they sing by the drums
And the trumpets of the sea.

Beaches kissed the sea
In white and black sands,
Where trees sleep on the hills
And mountains fade into the clouds.

Ocean sings with the sun,
Awaiting the warmth of its fires,
To give birth to the islands,
And for jungles to meet the seas.

Undersea Songs

Sacred stone down the lonely bay,
Singing chants of underwater tones.
Sanguine seas and suntan hues.
Sunken melodies of undersea choirs.

Sober waves hit the shores,
Serenading tunes of the fading day.
Sandy path uncovers when tides ebbs.
Sullen sunset sings its last goodbye.

Lights in the Shallow Seas

Adrift in its warm waters,
I heard the heartbeat of the sea
Through the waves of time
To show me its secrets at night.

Afloat on the shallow seas,
I gazed into the heavens
Watching the stars paint its face
Until I heard its whispers.

Waiting for the sun to rest,
I found myself in the dark waters,
And the light of the day
Had left the sea tonight.

Encircling around me
Are the fireflies of the sea,
Flickering after my strides
As the followed me.

Before the Night Came
Part IV

Twilight Stroll

Hand-painted skies,
Canvas in deep sapphire.
Amber etched by the horizon,
A panorama of darkness.

Soul Search

Oh, the light I gazed,
As crimson as embers!
When the trails ablaze,
Burnt in sparkling cinders.

Honey Amber Sunset

Almost home,
After a trip—alone.
Walked down the busy street,
Slow steps of sore feet.

Turquoise skies
As the sun bade goodbyes.
Amber rays on clouds cascade
In striking hues of marmalade.

Silhouette scene,
Canopies in seaweed green.
Overpass turns gravel gray—
Comes the night of May.

Before May Ends

The dry spells and short storms,
The humid sun and the short rains,
I heard its whispers and cries,
And its lullabies at dusk.

The clicking sounds moved time
By the waves of the seas,
Lighting up the ebony skies
And pulling me back to home.

The night called in purple-gray clouds
Along with the schools of squirrelfish,
Painting the horizon
in its blazing red scales.

I was left in its shadows
When its fires faded to welcome the stars.
I watched its last night
And reached the end of May.

Hours Before Midnight

And his sight
Was unto the firmament's collapse
And the god of Rome.
The guilt
And innocence.
From the blood,
Sunsets,
Verdure,
Oceans,
And into the twilight.
Intangible
And a disparity
From its lineage.
Only until the horses go forth,
Before the ram will come,
When the skies will split
And the twins will align.

Tender Fire

Blossom where stars hide,
Embracing sunset's cold warmth.
Tender fire on mountains and cave,
Serenading in silent flames.

Perch on blazing meadows,
Setting brazen torch afire.
Tepid strums in sedated tempo,
Dancing with sea breeze.

Dive on midnight sea,
Soaking into warm depths.
Piquant waters ebb and flood,
Engulfing with enchanting ballads.

Hush where beast reposes,
Dancing rhythmic wildfires.
Sudden flares of euphoric escapade,
Bursting in tight-lipped triumph.

Afternoon Sun

You ended like a sunset
Amongst the ships
That went past through time,
You knocked at my windows
To say goodbye,
And without a sound,
You slipped beyond the horizon.

Page 8034

I have come to the end of my days.
On this page, I stained with the pigments of life.
From ivory and into its darkest silhouettes—
Behind the fiery sunsets.

Engulfed in the warmth of the dying sun
And breathing in its orange hues.
Shades of blue cast into me
As it faded into its deepest black.

Home

Take me when you leave me
For I longed for your lullabies.
In your arms I will sleep
And in your cradle, I will return.

I kept your voice in a glass jar,
So when I will miss you,
I could open it once more
And hear you speak my name again.

Leave footprints along your way,
So I can walk back into you.
In your path I will run
And in your land, I will stay.

I will sing your name,
So when I will be gone,
Others will search for you
Until I they will find a home in you.

Scent of Home

The vessel swiftly flew forward,
Carrying the souls that longed for her.
Thunderstorms calmed and still,
Embracing her waist as she slept.
I see the familiar fields of the past—
The sea of grass, wide and vast.
Rolling hills dwarfed the dwellings
Like plump maiden breasts—
Fertile and abundant.
I am now home.
Sweet and grassy,
The scent of October
Surrounded my senses.
Freshly cut rice stalks wilt in joy—
Now fulfilled the wishes of their master.
Burning hay offered to bless the soil again—
Their souls reaching up to the heavens
In the deep scent of longing,
To come back home as storms.
To come and embrace her again.

The Sailors of the Skies

The Sailors of the Skies
Part V

Fireflies

I saw a fire that glows at flight.
An insect that is awake at night.
On the branches of a dead tree,
Everyone is flies for free.
They dance with the crickets,
And fly without tickets.
Everyone is on my back,
Always following my tracks.
Fireflies can shine in many ways,
But doesn't shine on day.
All join with the stars above,
With a flickering light of love.

Night Sky

I'll sleep
Under the blanket of stars,
Under the eyes of the moon,
And in the coldness of the night.

Nimbus and Luna

And the cloud
Formed a crescent,
With it horns
Pointing to the north.
Pale colors were in its belly,
Covered in thin cotton.
Gleaming in all its hues—
In a halo—
As it fades behind the cloud,
Moving northward.

The Moonlight

He is the shadow of the moon
And she is the rays of the sun.
She will kiss him night and day,
But he will sail unknown until it's dark.
He will wait from dusk till dawn,
And her gaze will be his morning.

Pirates of the Skies

Let's sail with my olden ship,
And delve into the waves of cirrus clouds.
Go along the cozy northern winds,
As we move closer to the stars.
Bathe with the moist midnight air,
And shiver by the cold moonlight.
Up above are the dark skies,
And below are treasures—yet unseen,
Gold flickering on the foothills and
Silvers gleaming by the rivers and the sea.

Counting Stars

I dreamt of stars,
Like the fruits of an apple tree,
As red as Mars
When I flew with a honeybee.

Starry Nights

I'll look up to find you,
And I'll paint in your darkest blue.
I'll watch under the flickering lights,
And I'll wait till I see these beautiful sights.

March Nights

Your lights were faint
When you stayed above me,
But the colors you paint,
Are in deep blue and gold like lapis lazuli.

Your air was humid
With a tinge of summer,
And the aroma was vivid
Like a vague scent of ochre.

A Night in April

Alone within
The dome of wonders,
Are innumerous specks of light
Shattered above the horizon.

Cotton-clouds afloat
Above inky clouds
And set behind the tall towers
Of gray clouds.

Random flashes
Of silent lightning
Lit on the far edges
Of the earth.

Evening star
In piercing gleam,
But not as to the golden crown
Of the night's full moon.

A Night in July

I heard your song,
Throbbing in warm colors.
Beside the pale moonlit clouds,
Your echoes resounding in orange flair.

City Stars

He gazed into the city skies,
His mind adrift by the late-night breeze,
And his thoughts dispersed with the stars.
Still and tranquil, the night deepened.

Midnight Lullabies

Under the mackerel sky,
Clouds licked the skies in an overcast,
And when the twilight ended,
The pack of gray clouds faded away.

Staring from the celestial sphere,
Pitch black and silent;
Searching for the sea of stars—
A whirlwind of constellations.

Stars slept on earth,
Playing silent evening tunes.
The elephantine, bulbous moon
Singing midnight lullabies.

The horizon dressed in clouds
Contrived in Elysian crown.
Heavenly dust thinly scattered—
Showering wishes and dreams.

The Galaxy in Our Eyes

I blankly stared
At the cloudy sky
For hours.
Waiting for a star
To greet me good night.
There might be
One or two
That I cannot see
By my window.
But, if it'll rain,
Let the cold wind
Send my warm hug,
Because there might be
Someone, too,
That looks at the stars like the way I do.

Deep Melodies

At nighttime,
The starry skies
Lulls me to sleep.
Deep,
Mellow melody.
Sleep.
Sleep.

Hibiscus

Paint me the darkest red
In the colors of dragon's breath,
As I lay in the thorns of black roses,
Left awake by the whispering pains.

Drown me in the midnight skies
In the hues of deep blue,
Like waves drifting me ashore,
Lost in the sound of my heartbeat.

Call the golden blackbirds
In the silhouette of the silver moon,
To rest on my shoulders,
Listening to the echoes of silence.

Cover me with your livid leaves
In the colors of black and blue,
Embracing my immortal flesh,
Until its roots reach my sorrows.

Before the Dawn Breaks

That sight
Of the jet-black sky
As it turns
Into shades of blue,
As the innumerable stars
Fades one by one.

Ylang-ylang

The fires had touched me.
Oh! The fires had touched me.

Midnight flowers bloomed at the heavens,
Enchanting the fishermen at sea:
Come.
Come.
Let us dine on land.

The new moon slept.
And the midnight flowers whispered:
Come.
Come.

Fishes dined by the light of men's torches.
Alluring.
Bedazzling sweet midnight fire.
Leap into the net of young men.
Fishes, rest unto the wooden boats.

The midnight flowers' sensuous fires
Pulling the fishermen from the sea:
Come.
Come.
Bring the fishes to me.

Its unseen fires had touched me—
And she died,
She died.
The midnight flowers died at day.

The Wildflower Trail
Part VI

Ideas

Did the men of the past
Felt something was missing,
Something was to be discovered
Or to invent?
There must be something—
Still vague—
Something unripe
And something not of today.
Why is there an ecstasy of the unknown?
A jolt of gut feelings?
Is it not the work of the hours?
In the dead of the night?
The mind has been playing games,
A puzzle with clues
That only lies through accidents and trials.
Have they failed more than a dozen?
Lost some good friends—
and sanity?
How many had stopped
And became nothing?
A multitude.
But can you count the men
That has persisted?
"Eureka! Eureka!",
They shouted.

The Masks We Made

Men hunt creatures for hides,
Covering its bodies for warmth,
Protecting from deadly parasites,
Or for camouflage from enemies or predators.

Leaves and loincloth laced around hips,
Began weaving crude and intricate fabrics,
Adorning with gold, silver and jewels
On mortal bodies as metaphors of beauty and
wealth.

Then men created masks of pretension
And cloaking its bodies from authenticity,
Escaping rejection from the majority,
Or blindly accepting what is wrong as right.

Strip all of what covers us,
Unclasping from the poisonous motives,
Bare from the lies that shield us,
And free from the pretense.

On Introversion

He distances himself
From everyone else,
As he drains too easily,
Unable to keep up with their energy.
He's active for a day,
And hibernate for another week,
Filling himself in energy
For another month of isolation.
He hydrates himself of silence,
Filling up the room with stillness,
Consuming webs of thoughts
And satiated in introspection.
He struggles to live
In a hyperactive world,
Thinking not of if he's to be liked,
But if at least one is in his liking.
He allows people
To fool him for their gain,
Watching their greedy faces
Covered in broken angelic masks.
He's bottling up emotions,
Dreading people and faking smiles,
Dying a bit inside,
For every emotional abuse he gets.
He's real,
Giving bloodshed to the oppressor,
Letting them taste regret—
Or he just stays away.
He disappears,
Staying away from stupidity,
Favoring moments solitude
Than being splattered with idiocy.

The Wildflower Trail

I went on a journey,
Chasing impossible dreams.
It was an uphill climb
That led me here.
Walking down the trail of wildflowers,
Finding a faster route.
I climbed above,
Searching for a better view.
I searched for a place,
But instead,
I found myself.
Amongst the blue sky,
I found peace.
I found solitude.
In the darkness,
I saw a different view.
I found a clearer view of my dream.

Daydreams

His mind was adrift
In an ocean of thoughts,
Wandering in its vastness
And lost in its beauty.
His eyes retire,
As the hours passed by.

How to Kill a Tree

Like a living tree,
With its roots anchoring
On the rocks below the ground
And its branches reaching the skies.

It bears good fruits,
For people to pick and share,
But only when its nourished
On the ground he stood.

Sever its roots—to oppress,
Deprive the soul from its food,
Let the leaves wilt
And its wood be burnt by fire.

To shave a man's head,
Are you not cutting a living tree?

Who Am I?

I am your imagination.
I am a speck of your daydreams.
I am a story you can't write.
I am the art you never made.
I am surreal and abstract, probably meaningless.
I am the ghost of your nightmares.
I am the shadow on a dark night.
I am idea you're afraid to discover.
I am hard and stubborn.
I am what you say to others.
I am the thunder in a storm.
I am the battles you never won.
I am the lies you make.
I am always right.
I am your tears and pain.
I am your anger and frustrations.
I am the past that haunts you.
I am the wound in your heart.
I am the sore in your body.
I am the dirt in your soul.
I am the step you didn't take.
But I realized that I am not.
I am the decision you carefully made.
I am the soul, not the dirt.
I am the strength that carried you.
I am what make your heart beats.
I am the lessons of the yesteryear.
I am your silence and peace.
I am your smiles and laughter.
I admit when I am wrong.
I am the truth you're holding on.
I am the fights you forgiven.
I am the warmth in the rain.
I am the word indescribable.
I am your Eureka moment.
I am fluid like gas and liquid.

I am what blocks the light.
I am the breath that saved your life.
I am a portrait, clear but means a thousand words.
I am the masterpiece in progress.
I am the pages of your book.
I am what's real.
I am you.

On Being Different

When no one believed in me—
And said that I should stop—
That moment,
I knew there was something
Extraordinary in me,
Something most minds
Can never comprehend.

Page 7975

Ten moons went by,
Past a score and a year,
All dreams changed—evolved.

Quirks I stood by,
Norms I don't adhere,
And questions still unsolved.

People ended in goodbye,
Slowly their tracks disappear,
And memories dissolved.

Let Boys Cry

If tears ne'er flow
Turns into crystals,
Like eyes of darkness—
Or a dull soot;
Murders the heart.
Cease to see, it
Fools the spirit or mind—
feeding hatred.
If tear ran out
Like rains
Left o' chaos;
But sun a 'glows,
Heals wounds—
Nor time can't—
Fuels life,
Builds ships.

Awake at Wee Hours

Hours after dusk,
Thinking over different things,
Appearing out from the dark—
Dissolving at daylight.

Awake before twilight,
Thinking of the incoming sun.
Idle for hours at nighttime,
Smashing clocks until morning.

Driving off the weekday blues
In random surge of imaginations.
Losing sleep on weeknights—
Convince me to sleep.

A night before it ends,
Before bursting into weekdays.
That period,
Awaiting sleep to come.

Late Night Thoughts

Late night thoughts visit me,
Spilled water and paint splashes;
I dance by the voices of my mind,
Ferocious, vibrant like sunsets.

Throbbing mind in sedated chaos,
Warm air and faint lights reflect;
I stare into the eruption of thoughts,
Tempting, harrowing like noises.

Silence awakens my soul,
Starry nights and jet-black skies;
I repose by the lullabies of the moon,
Tranquil, soothing like quiet rivers.

Vivid flashes in fiery visions,
Blank paper and worn brushes;
I paint in the melody of the night,
Dramatic, impassioned like thunder.

The Sleep Debts

When the sun was asleep,
My mind was on fire.
An elaborate web of ideas,
Fueling pen and papers.
When the sun peeked,
The bed whispered to me.
And after hours of sleep,
I think I needed more sleep.

The Sailors of the Skies

Olden Tales
Part VII

Of Old Age

The youth shall end,
When the eyes,
Now, never see beauty—
But gray hair.

Yesteryear

The elderly faded into the past,
And the kids of today
We're not even there in the yesteryear.
How each second swiftly pass by,
And time, slips away?

Storyteller

Old stories
Never written,
All, worth telling.
Birth,
Discovery,
And struggles.
Changing
With time,
Fades once untold.
Fragments
Of forgotten
Literature.

Art and the Beautiful Soul

(To Rose Maniego)
Summer—fiery as your flair,
Entrenched in the hats you wear;
Perilous thrills are your friends,
In solitude, your fervor ascends.

Kingfisher's Song

It sang in a glorious plea
As it perched on a high tree.
It has waited for the sight of the lost sea,
Leapt against the wind so swiftly.

Chafed

Fear not my dear,
Some yet things
Undone happen
A near.
For beats a clock,
Swings and again;
Yonder it grows
It runs amok.
Connects me unseen,
Binds in nothing?
Aren't we
Pain-stricken?
Berry red painted,
For stars taste also,
Swift it went
Two made not misled.

Hazy

One. Two. Three.
Let's close our eyes.
Four. Five. Six. Seven.
Then I woke up
It's not here.
Eight. Nine. Ten.
There it is!
Eleven. Twelve.
Now it's gone.
Thirteen. Fourteen. Fifteen.
It's getting dark.
Sixteen. Seventeen.
Let's fall asleep.
Eighteen. Nineteen.
It showed up.
Twenty. Twenty-one.
Now it's gone.

The Light That Never Came

A bird
With a dark and shiny coat
And a yellow belly.

His eyes
Full of strength
For good things tomorrow,
Or it may be fear
That there is no tomorrow
At all.

Was it it's curiosity?
That pulled him inside,
Or a light
That fooled his eyes.

There was everything inside—
New to him,
But nothing compared
To the outside.

From posts to walls
He fluttered with fear.
Giving its trust
Not to its feet,
But to the wings—
He could not fall.

Heartbeat grew stronger.
He was blind,
But he can hear
The outside,
Wailing for his return.

One by one
The light burnt out.

All he can see
Was nothing.

A lamp of home
He jumps towards,
But with his greatest grief—
It was a monster!

Emptied from everything,
He had only one thing left,
His life—to risk it all.

His wings
Fluttered in an eagle's strength.
But with no sight,
It was no use.

The last sound was a bang!

Green eyes
Held a bloody vessel—
Emptied to nothing.

Sleepy Cat

Untroubled feline of the urban avenue,
Dozed, unmoved on moonlit pavement.
Tainted air clouded the evening highway,
It slumbered, poised—the city's sovereign.

Deep Conversations

Maybe I could say hello everyday
And ask where your mind goes,
Or what world you'll escape to—
But you're a cat.

Maybe we could talk about dreams,
Goals, life, or causes you fight for,
Or how you sleep the frustrations away—
But you're a cat.

Maybe you could join me at late nights,
Stargazing by the silent rooftop,
And watching the clouds drift by—
But you're a cat.

Maybe we could laugh away the fears
And believe that dreams can come true
Or wait for the sun to rise—
I'll wait for you.

The Good Flatterer

Her eyes are set to see the good,
And a mouth to flatter
Both young and old.
She quips her best compliments
To make conversations fun,
And boasts the beauty unseen
Or the ageless of the wrinkled.
Her words are not to fool,
But are flowers so sweet and colorful.
She gives one to the budding singer,
And a bouquet to the youthful old man.
Her words are fresh flowers of spring,
To tame the hearts of the buzzing bees
And the butterflies of summer.
People aglow after her serenades,
Her heart blossoming in yellow daisies,
And her smiles as sweet as honey.
Her words are pure and not poison,
But the wise still knows what's real.

Golden Wolf

Golden wolf awaits me outside
Calling me not to follow its path,
In its vision, binds to my sight,
The cascade of mortal blood.

Its judgment weighs my soul,
Counts my value in pure gold,
It took three bars away from sight,
For I weigh less than I possess.

Its fur counts the value I hold,
In a wave of time it turned black,
And so, its color faded into sight
The perilous wolf becomes the night.

Its echoes lost in the silence
To leave my soul and be alive,
For I weigh no gold in its sight,
It calls its pack to guard my life.

Diverged Realities

On ordinary nights
My mind wanders,
As if my eyes are closed
Even when it's wide open.

It stares into a void,
Of a distance measured by time.
Where time is not in the past
Or in the future.
Rather, in a world unknown to me,
Or to my understanding.

A space where
There are just the depths
And the heavens.

Suddenly you are
On a rooftop.
Floating with the entities—
Without a background.

All the beauty
Of the imagination foretold.
Like the warmth
Of the late afternoon sun
Along the beaches,
Or on the hilltops,
Or it's lazy orange rays

From the silhouette of the western trees.
And above is a patch of blue skies
And a faint white cloud.

The touch of the nostalgic breeze,

The Sailors of the Skies

And the earthy burnt dust
In the air,
As I lay with the grasses.

Sometimes you are on a treetop,
When the white birds return to the south.
Hastily the cerulean sky turns crimson,
Blazing on the edges of your eyesight.

One-after-another
The stars begin to appear.
How are you so clueless?
Of how you lived
On the other world.

Then you wake up dying
To talk to me
from the different universe.

Fading Dreams

Stargazing tree bears none,
Deprived of the desires
To raise its branches to the skies,
Unable to taste the stars.

In its dreams, it burns bright
In desires and hopes,
With its branches into the skies
Bearing new moons and stars.

But its dreams died in the heavens,
Along with its leaves
Perishing by the wild winds,
To lay asleep forever.

Thunder awakens its illusions,
Losing the fires in the heavens,
And clouds lined the horizons,
Waiting to fall on earth.

Graves of the Poor

I die in the graves of many,
And as beautiful as a day,
I watch the body crumbles
Until its life is gone.

For a stranger to this land,
I must carry silver and gold
In my pocket and my face
If I fear myself to die in pain.

If I own nothing, then I—
I own a grave to rest with the poor,
Whose life is uncounted,
But death is tallied.

If by chance a heart give,
A living soul be saved again,
But the pain to watch the poor,
Then I die in the graves of many.

Things We Often Forget

If you came to a thought
Why there's seems
No special events
Happening in your life,
Think about the thirsty,
But no water to drink,
The hungry but no food to eat,
The tired,
But no house to live in,
And the sick,
But no one seems to help.
You may be physically burdened
And emotionally broken,
But it shall pass,
Better things await.
That beat of your heart,
It's a sign that you
Shall accomplish
More good things in life.
You've received countless blessings,
Take time to see how special
And blessed you are,
Share that blessings to others.

Every Night It Plays

The kids are on their beds,
The kids are not asleep.
She shouts, he's forbidding,
Glasses breaks and plate shatters.

The scene replays at night,
The scene that they hate.
She shouts, he's yelling,
Glasses breaks and plate shatters.

The man wastes his life,
The man continued his vices.
She waits, he's away,
Time passes by, kids grow up.

The man left the family,
The man builds another home,
She waits, he's gone,
Time passes by, kids grow up.